CHARLES LETTS · Letts · FOUNDED 1796

EARLY LEARNING W

For three- to five-year-olds

More, More!

Story by Pie Corbett
Activities by David Bell, Pie Corbett
Geoff Leyland and Mick Seller

Illustrations by Diann Timms

Baby had learnt a word.
'Would you like an orange?'
'More,' called Baby.

Look at the oranges in the picture.

Do you know what oranges smell like?
See if you can find one and smell it.

What does it feel like to touch?
Is the skin smooth or rough?

Ask Mum or Dad to cut the orange
open for you.
Does the inside look the same as the outside?
Does it smell the same?

‘Would you like a biscuit?’
‘More,’ called Baby.

Baby is in the high chair.
Is the high chair taller than Mum?
Is it taller than Jenny?

Is there a high chair in your home?
Is it taller or shorter than you?

Look around the room.
What is the tallest thing you can see?
What is the shortest?

‘Would you like some cake?’

‘More,’ called Baby.

The cakes in the picture are different colours and shapes.
Do you know what they are called?

Find some coloured modelling clay and see if you can make some pretend cakes which look like the ones in the picture. You will need several different colours of clay.

‘More’ was the only word Baby could say.

Mum said it could get you into trouble.

When have you been in trouble?
What happened?

Ask your mum and dad what your first word was.

Do you know any babies that are just beginning to speak?
What can they say?

Suppose someone said,
'Would you like a drink?'
and you kept saying 'More'.

How many drinking glasses can you see?

How many mugs can you see?

How many cups can you see?

Suppose someone said,
'Would you like a pet?'
and you kept saying 'More'.

Would you like to have all these animals as pets?

Which of the animals would make good pets?

Talk about what the animals would eat, how they move and how big they are.

See if you can find the biggest animal in the picture, then the smallest one.

Suppose someone said,
'Would you like a piggy back?'
and you kept saying 'More'.

Imagine that you had to sort out all these pigs.
How would you do it?

Would you sort them by colour?
What colours can you see?
How many black and white pigs are there?
How many pink pigs are there?
Are there more pink than black and white pigs, or more black and white than pink pigs?
How many more are there?
Or would you sort the pigs by size?

Suppose someone said,
'Would you like an ice-cream?'
and you kept saying 'More'.

Ask your mum and dad to help you make an ice balloon by stretching a balloon over the cold water tap and partly filling it with water.

Tie the balloon and put it in an empty ice-cream container in the freezer for two days.

When you take it out, cut the balloon away and put your ice balloon into a bowl of warm water.

Talk about what it looks like.
What does it remind you of?
How would you tell somebody about what it looks like?

When Mum went to work,
Yasmin and her Mum, Jamilla,
came round to look after
Jenny and Baby.

What job do you think Jenny's Mum does?
What job do you think her Dad does?
Does Jamilla have a job?

What jobs would you like to do when you are older?

Talk about all the people who visit your house and what their jobs are.

They went to the shops to get something for their tea.

Do you have any shops near you?
If you walk to the shops, how long
does it take you?

If you go by car, ask the driver to
tell you how far it is. Is it less
than a mile or more than a mile?

What sort of shop is nearest to where
you live? What's your favourite shop?
Talk about what it sells.

They bought some bread,
baked beans, apples and milk.

All the items in the shops have prices. Do you recognise any of the prices?

How much does a tin of baked beans cost? Do you have enough money in your piggy bank to buy a tin of beans?

What would you buy in the shop if you were shopping?

Baby ran round the shop
shouting, 'More, more, more!'

Next time you go shopping, help Mum to write the shopping list.

You could write down everything you need or you could draw some of the things you are going to buy.

Jamilla was cross.

She told Baby to stop being silly.

Can you spot the labels on any of the tins?

Make a collection of labels from tins and packets of food that you like.
You could stick them on to a poster.

See if you can recognise the packets next time you go shopping.
Try to spot the names on the packets.

But Baby was really naughty and knocked over all the tins...

Look at those tins rolling away!

If you knocked over a pile of bananas, would they roll away?

Make a slope and roll these things down it:
a banana, a tin, a toy car.
Which one rolls the best?
You could try rolling some other things down the slope.

This time Jamilla was very cross.

She said,
'Would you like a smacked bottom?'

Baby ran away laughing and
shouting, 'More! More!'.

Could you make a menu for your favourite meal?

Think about what you would like to eat, draw the different foods and then ask Mum or Dad to help you write their names beside them.

When you go to a café, ask someone to show you the menu.

It tells what you can eat and drink and how much it will cost.
See if you can find the names of your favourite foods and drinks.

Activity Notes

Pages 2-3 This activity involves close observation of an orange using smell, touch and careful looking. Familiar objects can suddenly become fascinating when studied in this detailed way.
Extend the activity by cutting open two oranges in different ways: 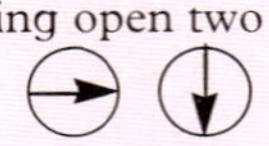
Do the insides look different when you do this?

Pages 4-5 Children begin to develop an understanding of measures such as height, weight and length by making simple comparisons. When they do, encourage the use of terms such as 'taller than' and 'shorter than'.

Pages 6-7 Encourage the accurate naming of the colours and shapes of the cakes. Ask what colour the cakes would be inside and discuss their taste. You could buy some small buns, rolls or fancy cakes. Cut them open and look at the insides. Talk about the patterns, shapes and colours.

Pages 8-9 Talking about personal experiences can help children develop a sense of sequence. Taking an interest in how language develops and how we use talk is an important part of learning about language. It is fun to tape-record your children and let them hear how they sounded when they were much younger.

Pages 10-11 Children need to be able to distinguish between items if they are to count one object at a time. Encourage them to point to, touch or physically move individual items as they are counted.

Pages 12-13 The questions develop the ideas of similarities and differences in movement, diet, size and habit. You could continue this by putting the animals into groups together, eg, animals which eat meat, hop, have fur, are bigger than me, eat grass, live in jungles and so on. This initial classification could be followed by drawing the sets of animals.

Pages 14-15 As children begin to count objects, they realise that there can be more of one item than another. Begin with simple guesses, eg, 'Do you think there are more apples than oranges?'. Then count the objects and children will soon appreciate that numbers represent different values.

Pages 16-17 The ice balloon is an unusual way of stimulating scientific thinking in young children. A wide range of tactile experiences and vocabulary will develop from it.
Try making ice blocks of different sizes and shapes. Float them in a small bowl of warm water. Talk together about your observations. Which shapes and sizes melt the quickest?

Pages 18-19 Jamilla is a friend of the family. She is also a child-minder. This activity draws children's attention to the world of work, in particular those who help us. With your child, you could draw and label pictures of visitors to the house.

Pages 20-21 Young children have very little idea of long distances and therefore, at this stage, it is only possible to introduce the appropriate language and the idea of relative distances, eg, a mile is much longer than a metre. Talk about distances of common journeys, so that children begin to have an idea of what units of distance mean.

Pages 22-23 As children go shopping, encourage them to recognise numbers or read prices. This can be related to any sums of money children happen to be carrying at the time so that relevant vocabulary such as 'more than' or 'less than' can be introduced.

Pages 24-25 Let your child write their own shopping list. At first the writing may be scribble, later on letter shapes will appear. Show your child how to write their own name.

Pages 26-27 Sometimes the first words that children recognise and read are the most familiar - such as the brand name of their favourite cereal. Draw your child's attention to a few special labels or signs. For instance, a child might easily spot the word 'Services' on the motorway if you point it out to them over a period of time.

Pages 28-29 Some objects are better rollers than others. Talk about the shapes of each object in the collection. Measure how far they roll using footsteps or handspans. Now investigate whether the best shapes for rolling are also the best shapes for stacking. You could use bananas, apples, toy cars, empty drinks cans, boxes or building blocks.

Pages 30-31 Either write the names of the foods for your child or let them have a go. It doesn't matter if at this stage their writing is just scribble or a line of letter shapes. Next time you eat out, point out the menu and some of the items on it that you know your child likes.